Contents

Amazing Animals

The world is full of amazing animals. You might know a lot about some animals – you might even live with some. Other animals might be a bit more of a mystery. Do you ever wonder about them?

Do you ever think about why some animals have big ears or a tail? Maybe you want to know why they purr or waddle? Read on to find the answers to some of these questions and more.

Why Do Dogs Wag Their Tails?

Why do dogs wag their tails? If you think it's because they are friendly, you're right! However, this is not the only reason. Dogs wag their tails to tell us how they feel.

Often, a wagging tail means "I'm happy to see you" or "I like playing with you". Short and slow tail wags can mean the dog is pleased and happy.

Dogs will also wag their tails to tell us they feel worried, scared or even angry. Short and fast tail wags can mean the dog is feeling **aggressive**.

Puppies don't wag their tails from birth. This is something they start to do at about six weeks old. Puppies wag their tails when they come up to their mother to be fed. They also wag their tails at other puppies in the litter. Let's look at what some different tail wags mean.

High in the air and waving slowly

This dog feels in charge.
It is ready to **defend** its territory.

Low and wagging quickly

This dog feels shy and maybe a bit scared. It is saying, "I know you're the boss!"

Straight out and wagging

This dog is feeling friendly and **relaxed**. This is how a dog might look when it sees its owner.

High and wagging fast

This dog is friendly and excited.
It might want to play with you!

Why Do Cats Purr?

Have you heard a cat purr? Most people love this soft, humming sound and find it very relaxing to listen to.

Cats purr when they are happy and **contented**. Some cats even have a special purr for their owners that means, “Feed me, please!”

Did You Know?

Cats purr when they breathe in and out. The muscles in the cat’s voice box vibrate (shake) when air passes through.

However, there is more to purring than meets the ear. Cats also purr when they are scared or hurt. Sick and injured cats often purr. It is thought that this helps them to feel better and to calm down.

Kittens purr soon after birth. They start purring when they are being fed by their mother.

As they get older, cats purr when they play. Sometimes, they purr when they see other cats. This means they are being friendly and want to come closer.

People often give a big smile to someone when they want something. When a cat wants something, it rubs against your legs and purrs.

Why do cats purr for different reasons? Well, purring for a cat is a bit like smiling is for a person – one action is used to mean different things. We smile when we are happy, but sometimes we smile when we are nervous, too.

Why Do Camels Have Humps?

Camel humps are full of water – right? No – wrong! Camel humps are full of fat.

Camels can't always find food in the desert so they eat as much as they can, whenever they can. The food they don't need is stored in their humps as fat.

When a camel can't find food, its body uses some of its stored fat for **energy**.

Did You Know?

People store fat, too. It spreads out under their skin.

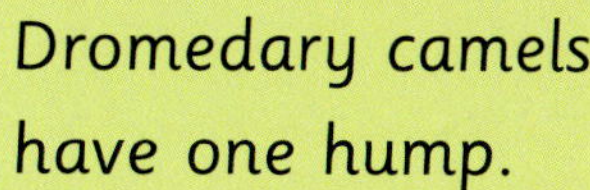

Bactrian camels have two humps.

Camels do not store water in their humps, but they can drink huge amounts of water. They use it up very slowly.

Why Do Penguins Waddle?

Have you seen penguins walk? They take very short steps and rock from side to side. You might think their waddle is funny, but penguins are not trying to make you laugh. So, why do they waddle?

*The penguin's wings are flippers for swimming. Its feet are like **rudders** on a ship. They steer the penguin through water.*

Penguins are birds but they do not fly. They spend a lot of time in the water. A penguin's body is solid, with a short neck and a round head. It has short legs and big feet. This type of body is good for swimming, but it is not so good for walking!

Penguins can only take tiny steps because of their short legs. It takes a lot of energy for them to put one foot in front of the other. Rocking from side to side is the easiest way to walk. Waddling also helps penguins keep their balance so they don't fall sideways.

Can you walk like a penguin?

1. Stand up straight with your arms by your sides.
2. Turn out your hands.
3. Put your heels together and turn out your toes.
4. Start to waddle!

Don't lift your up feet too much and remember to take small steps!

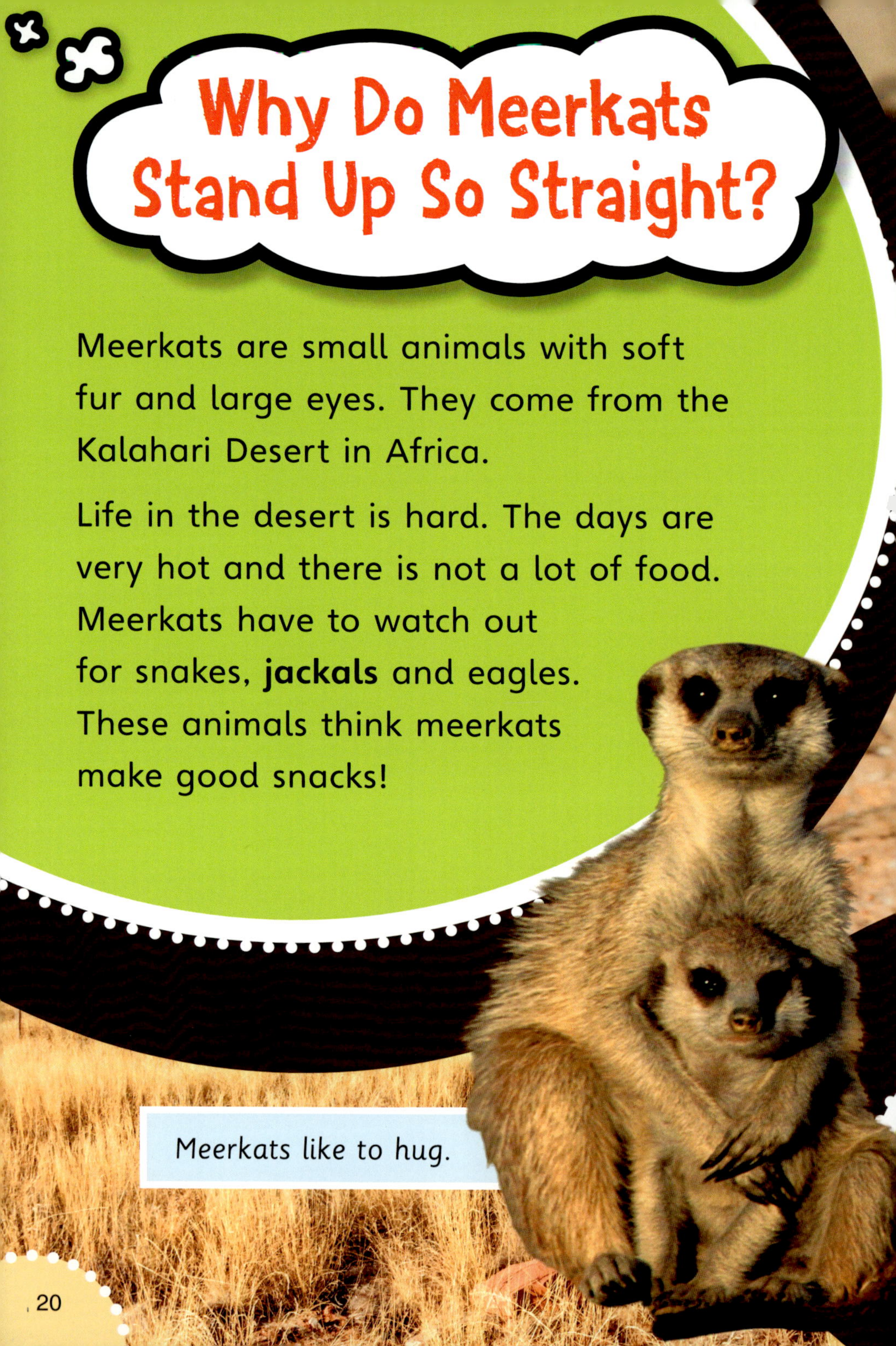

Why Do Meerkats Stand Up So Straight?

Meerkats are small animals with soft fur and large eyes. They come from the Kalahari Desert in Africa.

Life in the desert is hard. The days are very hot and there is not a lot of food. Meerkats have to watch out for snakes, **jackals** and eagles. These animals think meerkats make good snacks!

Meerkats like to hug.

Did You Know?

A group of meerkats is called a mob or a gang.

To help them keep safe, meerkats live in large family groups. These tiny animals work together to keep their group safe – they like to stick together!

Each meerkat has an important job to do. Some look for food and others look after the babies. One very important job is to look out for danger. This is the job of the **sentry**.

The sentry watches while the other meerkats look for food. The sentry stands up on its hind legs. Sometimes, it finds a high spot on the ground or climbs a tree so it can see for a long way. The sentry makes a loud beeping sound if it sees something scary. Then, all the meerkats run to safety.

Why Do Elephants Have Big Ears?

In the story *Dumbo*, a young elephant flies when he flaps his ears. Elephants can't really fly like this but their ears are still pretty cool. In fact, that is why they have big ears – to keep them cool!

Elephants live in hot places. It can be hard for them to cool down when they are hot, but they get rid of heat through their big ears.

Elephant ears are a bit like a cooling fan. Elephants have lots of blood **vessels** in their ears. Blood vessels are like tubes that carry blood around the body.

Did You Know?

The blood vessels in an elephant's ears make a pattern. This pattern is different for each elephant – just like a person's fingerprints.

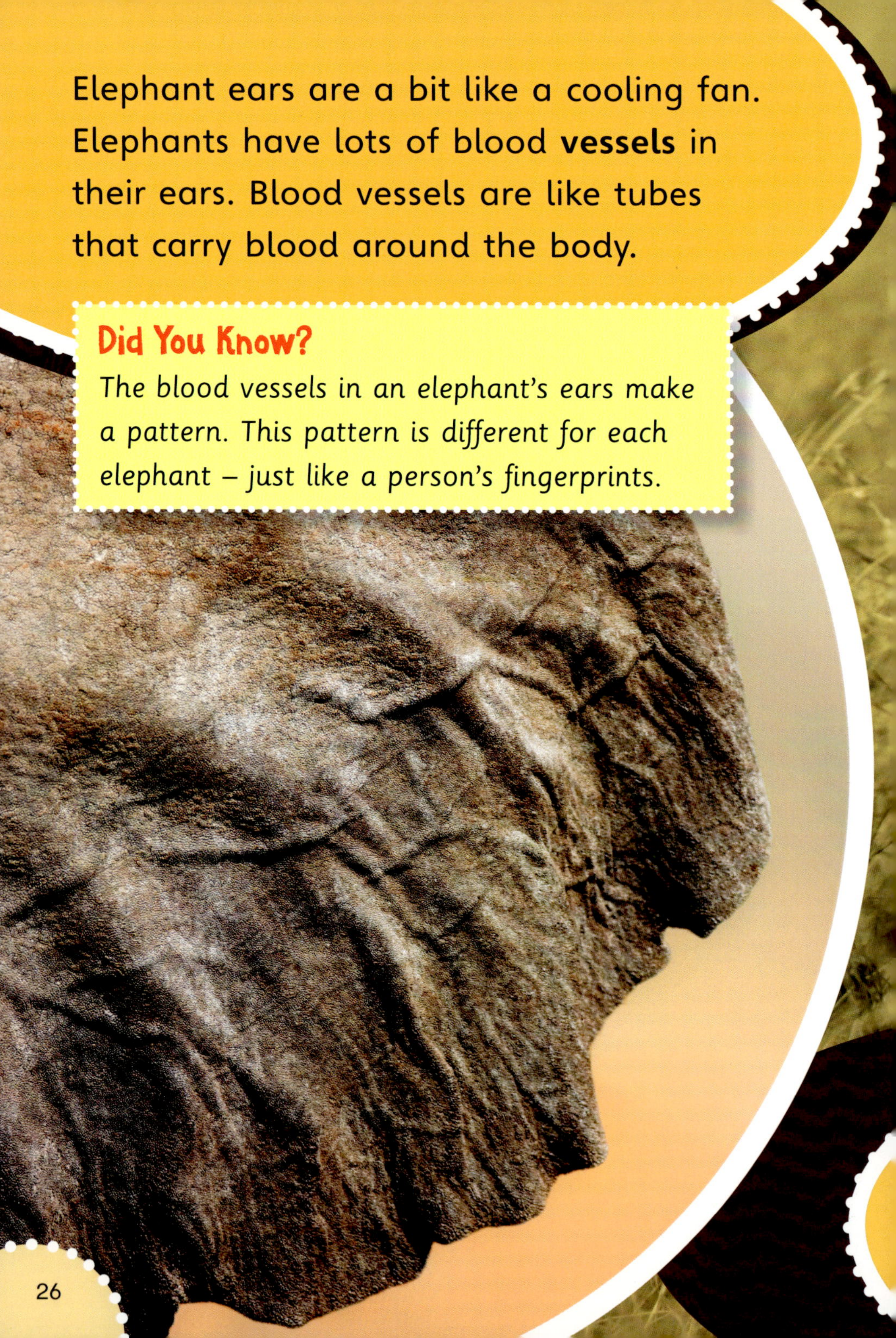

Did You Know?

Elephants come from Africa and India. African elephants have larger ears because it is hotter in Africa.

The blood is cooled down when an elephant flaps its ears. This makes the rest of the elephant cooler, too.

Dear Animal Expert,

Why do *sea otters* hold hands?

Sea otters live in groups. They spend most of their time in the water — even to eat and sleep! When they are resting or sleeping, they hold hands so they don't float off by themselves. A group of otters is called a raft.

Dear Animal Expert,
Why do dolphins swim in front of boats?
Are they surfing for fun?

Maybe! Boats make waves when they move through the water. Dolphins sometimes like to swim in front of a boat and get pushed by the wave. This is called “bow riding”. They seem to do this for fun – a bit like body surfing. The waves also help dolphins swim faster. It might be a way of “catching a lift” when they are tired!

Dear Animal Expert,
Why do chimpanzees pick through each other's hair?

Chimpanzees like to **groom** each other. This is when they go through each other's hair and get rid of dirt, insects and bits of plants. They like it so much they will do it for about an hour each day! Grooming helps them to keep clean, but it is also a way to be friendly. It makes chimpanzees feel relaxed and happy.

Dear Animal Expert,

Why do Koalas sleep so much? Are they lazy?

Koalas sleep and rest for up to 22 hours a day. They are pretty sleepy! It's not because they're lazy, though. Koalas don't get much energy from their food – eucalyptus leaves. This means that they have to save their energy as much as possible, so they sleep for most of the time. They spend a few hours eating each day and only a short time moving around.

Glossary

aggressive likely to attack

contented happy; happy with how things are

defend protect someone or something against an attack

energy strength to do things

groom clean

jackal wild dog

relaxed calm and at ease

rudders pieces of wood or metal at the back of a boat that control steering